LOOK INSIDE
CROSS-SECTIONS
RESCUE
VEHICLES

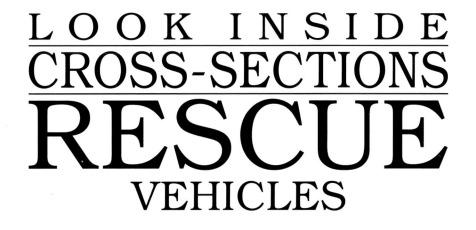

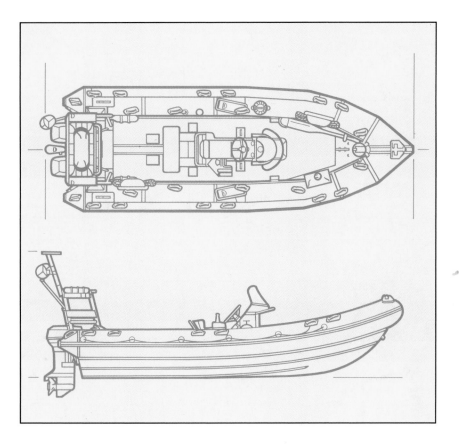

LOOK INSIDE
CROSS-SECTIONS
RESCUE
VEHICLES

ILLUSTRATED BY
HANS JENSSEN

WRITTEN BY
LOUISA SOMERVILLE

DK

DORLING KINDERSLEY
LONDON • NEW YORK • STUTTGART

A DORLING KINDERSLEY BOOK

Art Editor Dorian Spencer Davies
Designer Sharon Grant, Sara Hill
Senior Art Editor C. David Gillingwater
Project Editor Constance Novis
Senior Editor John C. Miles
U.S. Editor Camela Decaire
Production Louise Barratt

First American edition, 1995
2 4 6 8 10 9 7 5 3 1
Published in the United States
by Dorling Kindersley Publishing, Inc.,
95 Madison Avenue, New York, New York 10016

Library of Congress Cataloging - in - Publication Data

Somerville, Louisa.
Rescue vehicles / artist, Hans Jenssen and Alan Austin: author,
Louisa Somerville. – – 1st American ed.
p. cm. – (Look inside cross-sections)
Includes index.
ISBN 1-56458-879-3
1. Emergency vehicles – – Juvenile literature.
[1. Emergency vehicles.]
I. Jenssen, Hans, 1963- ill.
II. Austin, Alan, ill. III. Title. IV. Series.
TL235.8.S64 1995

629. 04 – – dc20   94 – 23756
                                         CIP
                                         AC

Reproduced by Dot Gradations, Essex
Printed and bound by Proost, Belgium

CONTENTS

POLICE CAR

Flashing light reflector

To CATCH ESCAPED CRIMINALS or handle an incident in which suspects may be armed and dangerous, many police forces operate K-9 units equipped with specially trained dogs. Sometimes the cars used by these officers are standard police models with a specially built compartment for the dog, like the example shown here. The furry deputy has a space to himself, and the officer he works with sits up front with all the hardware. Together they are a formidable team in the war against crime!

A strapping suspect
Because the only passenger seat in this car is in the front beside the officer, suspects under arrest are restrained with handcuffs and a large leather strap. This is carried in the trunk when not needed.

Trunk lid

K-9 unit identification symbol

Rear window

Dog compartment

K-9 collar badge

Leather strap to restrain suspects

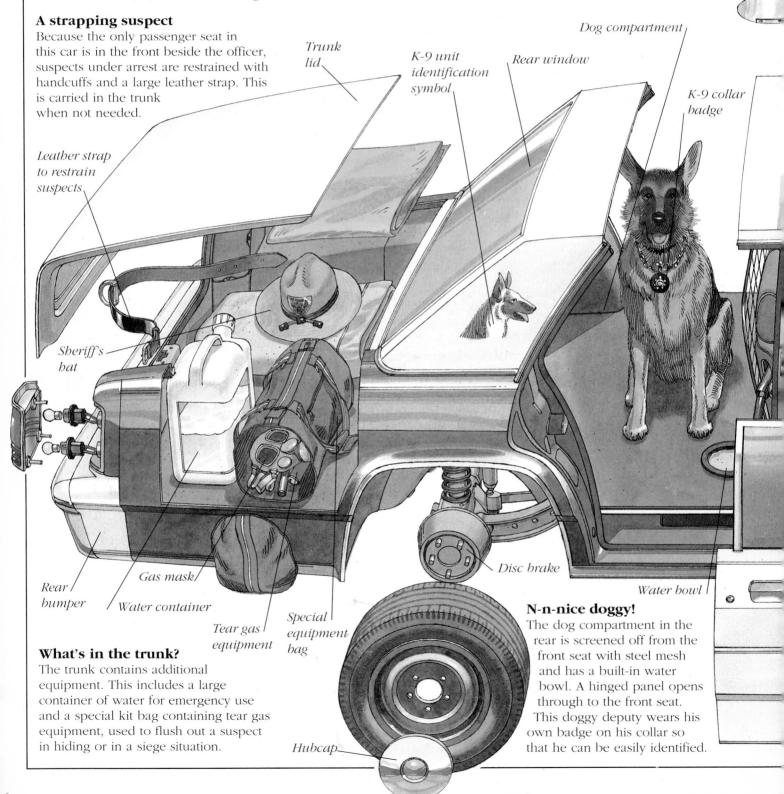

Sheriff's hat

Rear bumper

Gas mask

Water container

Tear gas equipment

Special equipment bag

Disc brake

Water bowl

Hubcap

What's in the trunk?
The trunk contains additional equipment. This includes a large container of water for emergency use and a special kit bag containing tear gas equipment, used to flush out a suspect in hiding or in a siege situation.

N-n-nice doggy!
The dog compartment in the rear is screened off from the front seat with steel mesh and has a built-in water bowl. A hinged panel opens through to the front seat. This doggy deputy wears his own badge on his collar so that he can be easily identified.

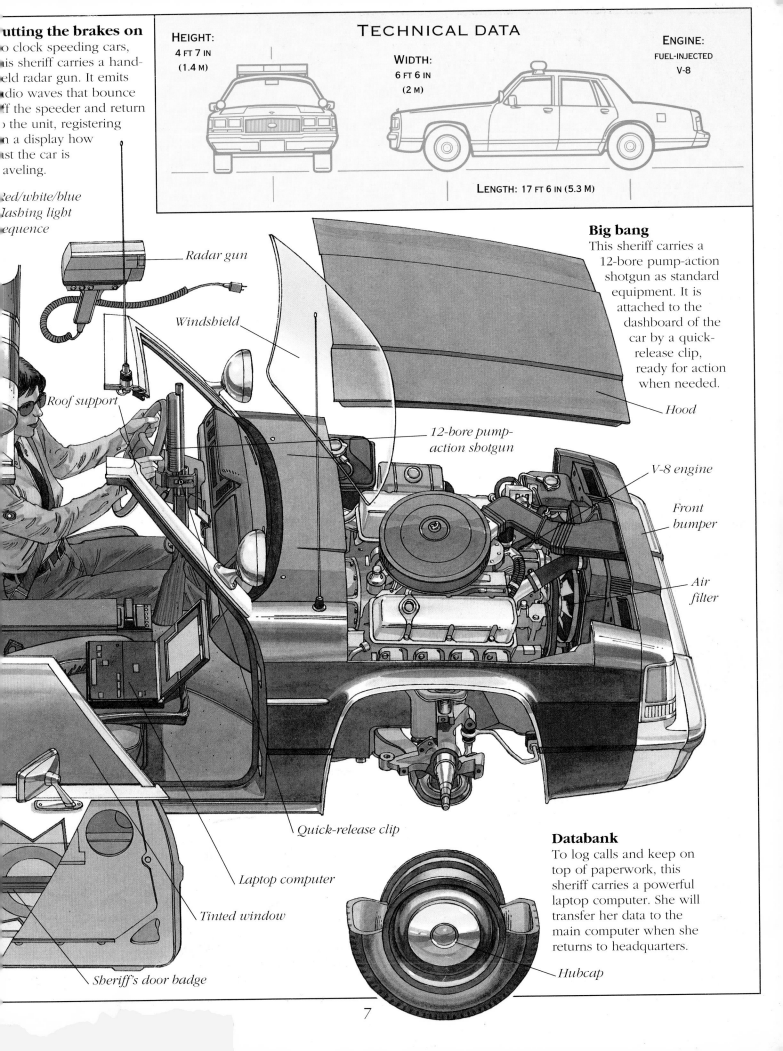

Putting the brakes on

To clock speeding cars, this sheriff carries a hand-held radar gun. It emits radio waves that bounce off the speeder and return to the unit, registering on a display how fast the car is traveling.

Red/white/blue flashing light sequence

TECHNICAL DATA

HEIGHT:
4 FT 7 IN
(1.4 M)

WIDTH:
6 FT 6 IN
(2 M)

ENGINE:
FUEL-INJECTED
V-8

LENGTH: 17 FT 6 IN (5.3 M)

Radar gun

Windshield

Roof support

Big bang

This sheriff carries a 12-bore pump-action shotgun as standard equipment. It is attached to the dashboard of the car by a quick-release clip, ready for action when needed.

Hood

12-bore pump-action shotgun

V-8 engine

Front bumper

Air filter

Quick-release clip

Laptop computer

Tinted window

Databank

To log calls and keep on top of paperwork, this sheriff carries a powerful laptop computer. She will transfer her data to the main computer when she returns to headquarters.

Hubcap

Sheriff's door badge

7

FIRE ENGINE

Flashing light

Siren

Tough customer
The Bronto Skylift has a sturdy steel body strong enough to cope with the toughest situations. The body is bolted onto the chassis (frame). Various makes of chassis are used.

Radio to headquarters

Cradle to support folded boom

WHEN FIRE BREAKS OUT at the top of a tall building, you need an aerial ladder platform fire engine, such as the Bronto Skylift shown here, to deal with it. With lights flashing and siren blaring, this versatile engine races through the streets, weaving in and out of traffic. Once at the scene, its long arm raises firefighters high up in a protective cage to give them the best view of the problem – and to take them near enough to rescue people and fight the fire.

Windshield

Driver's seat

Flashing front light

Boom operator
The booms are operated from a control panel at the turntable. The boom operator and the firefighter in the cage keep in touch with each other by an intercom. The person in the cage may have a better overall view of the situation from high up and can help the boom operator guide the arms to the right place.

Batteries

Steering linkage

Radiator

Front bumper

Wheel

Engine

Rescued
People who have been rescued can scramble down a ladder attached to the side of the boom. There is a safety rail so they can't fall. From the turntable there is a drop-down ladder so they can get down to the ground safely.

Engine fan

Four legs
Four outrigger legs keep the truck steady when the booms are raised. Each leg can be adjusted so that the truck stands firm on uneven ground. Foot plates help spread the weight.

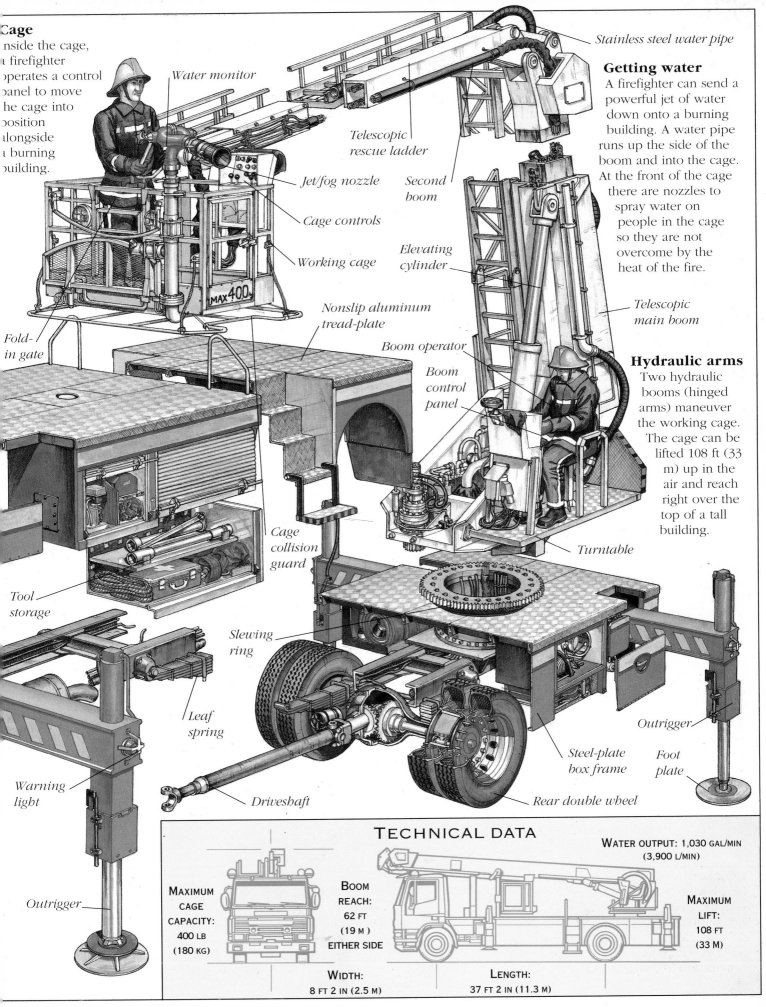

Cage
Inside the cage, a firefighter operates a control panel to move the cage into position alongside a burning building.

Water monitor

Telescopic rescue ladder

Second boom

Jet/fog nozzle

Cage controls

Working cage

Stainless steel water pipe

Getting water
A firefighter can send a powerful jet of water down onto a burning building. A water pipe runs up the side of the boom and into the cage. At the front of the cage there are nozzles to spray water on people in the cage so they are not overcome by the heat of the fire.

Elevating cylinder

Boom operator

Boom control panel

Telescopic main boom

Hydraulic arms
Two hydraulic booms (hinged arms) maneuver the working cage. The cage can be lifted 108 ft (33 m) up in the air and reach right over the top of a tall building.

Fold-in gate

Nonslip aluminum tread-plate

Turntable

Tool storage

Cage collision guard

Slewing ring

Leaf spring

Outrigger

Foot plate

Warning light

Driveshaft

Steel-plate box frame

Rear double wheel

Outrigger

TECHNICAL DATA

MAXIMUM CAGE CAPACITY: 400 LB (180 KG)

BOOM REACH: 62 FT (19 M) EITHER SIDE

WATER OUTPUT: 1,030 GAL/MIN (3,900 L/MIN)

MAXIMUM LIFT: 108 FT (33 M)

WIDTH: 8 FT 2 IN (2.5 M)

LENGTH: 37 FT 2 IN (11.3 M)

FIREBOAT

FIGHTING FIRES ON A WATERFRONT or a ship can be tricky and dangerous. That's why many cities situated on a river or harbor maintain fireboats. Painted bright red and driven by powerful engines, fireboats contain both firefighting and lifesaving equipment, and are equal to just about any emergency on water. Their main weapons are powerful water cannons called fire monitors. When the pumps are turned on, the monitors blast strong columns of water or foam at a blaze. With an unlimited supply of water available, firefighting activities can last as long as fuel to run the pumps holds out.

Lifesavers
The casualty room at the stern can take six stretcher cases. There is also a portable operating table so doctors or paramedics can carry out emergency surgery and other lifesaving procedures. Lockers around the room hold drugs, dressings, and other medical equipment.

Bright idea
An emergency lighting mast holds six 2,000-watt lights to illuminate the scene of an incident. It can be raised 33 ft (10 m).

A tight spot
At the stern, a motorized dinghy sits in a launching crane, ready to swoop out and rescue casualties from spaces too tight for the large boat. The launching gantry has a winch to retrieve the boat after use.

Daring divers
Divers assist the boat's crew with underwater rescues. A folding staircase hanging over the side helps them clamber in and out of the water.

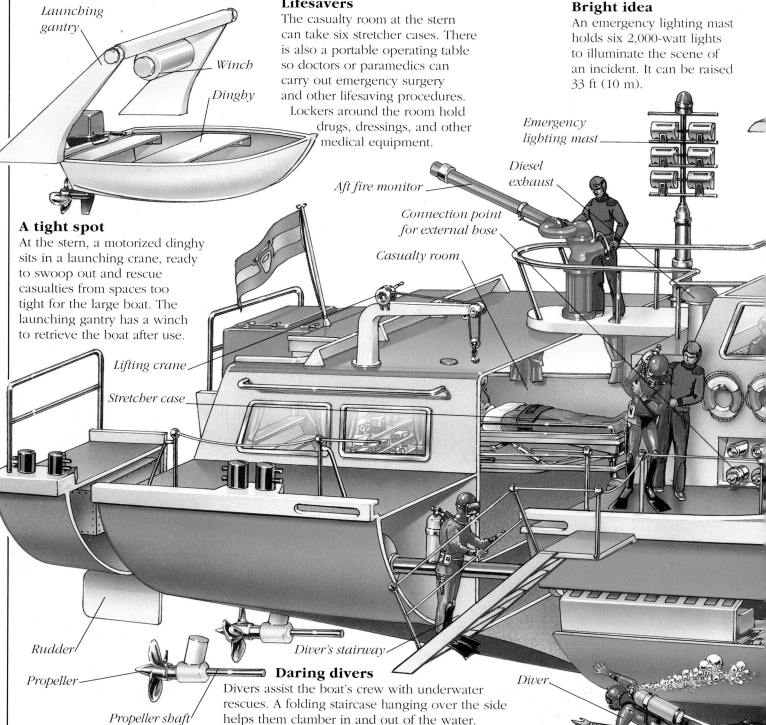

Launching gantry

Winch

Dinghy

Lifting crane

Stretcher case

Rudder

Propeller

Propeller shaft

Diver's stairway

Aft fire monitor

Connection point for external hose

Casualty room

Diesel exhaust

Emergency lighting mast

Diver

Fabulous foam

Firefighters use fire-retardant foam to put out fires involving substances that spraying water would only spread, such as burning oil. The foam smothers the fire by cutting off its supply of oxygen.

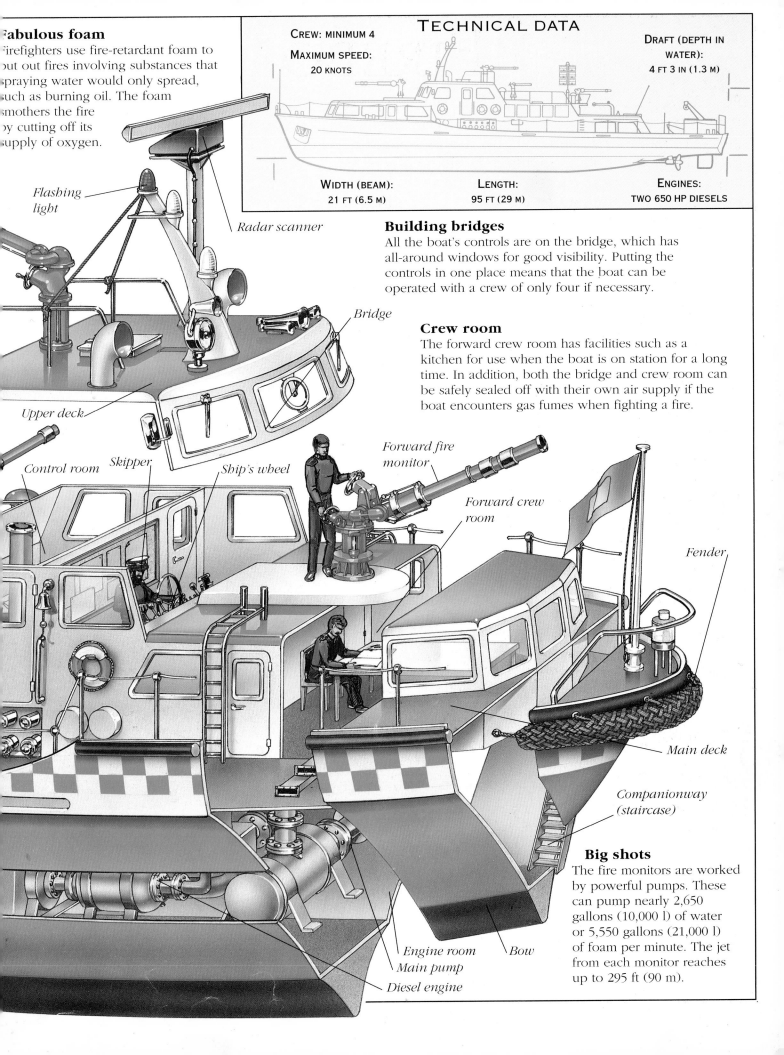

Flashing light

Radar scanner

Upper deck

Control room *Skipper* *Ship's wheel*

Bridge

TECHNICAL DATA

CREW: MINIMUM 4		DRAFT (DEPTH IN WATER):
MAXIMUM SPEED: 20 KNOTS		4 FT 3 IN (1.3 M)
WIDTH (BEAM): 21 FT (6.5 M)	LENGTH: 95 FT (29 M)	ENGINES: TWO 650 HP DIESELS

Building bridges

All the boat's controls are on the bridge, which has all-around windows for good visibility. Putting the controls in one place means that the boat can be operated with a crew of only four if necessary.

Crew room

The forward crew room has facilities such as a kitchen for use when the boat is on station for a long time. In addition, both the bridge and crew room can be safely sealed off with their own air supply if the boat encounters gas fumes when fighting a fire.

Forward fire monitor

Forward crew room

Fender

Main deck

Companionway (staircase)

Big shots

The fire monitors are worked by powerful pumps. These can pump nearly 2,650 gallons (10,000 l) of water or 5,550 gallons (21,000 l) of foam per minute. The jet from each monitor reaches up to 295 ft (90 m).

Engine room
Main pump
Diesel engine
Bow

INSHORE BOAT

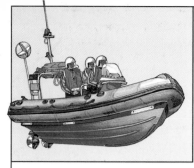

WITHIN FIVE MINUTES OF THE "SHOUT," an inshore rescue crew launches their inflatable lifeboat from the beach. Since they came into operation, inflatable lifeboats, such as this Atlantic 21, have proven to be excellent craft for handling inshore rescue operations – they're tough yet maneuverable enough to work close to rocks or in shallow conditions without running aground.

Seating
Seating is arranged in a T-shape to give the crew maximum all-around visibility. Each seat position has a pair of foot straps fitted to the deck.

Capsized!
If the boat capsizes, capsize lamps light up the underside of the upturned lifeboat so the crew and survivors are not left in total darkness. A crew member activates a gas bottle to inflate the righting air bag, stored in the boat's stern, and the lifeboat rolls back upright in just a few seconds. All the engine parts and electrical equipment are waterproofed so the engine will still work, even after capsizing.

Fuel
Two 22-gallon (82-l) stainless steel fuel tanks are installed below deck. They are encased in foam and painted with waterproof paint to make sure water cannot get in. On full tanks, the boat is capable of running for three hours at its maximum speed of 29 knots – long enough for complicated rescue situations.

First aid
Rescue boats carry a variety of first aid equipment, including a watertight first aid kit, mouth-to-mouth resuscitation aid, a space blanket, and life jackets for two extra passengers.

Inflatable sponson
The lifeboat has an inflatable sponson (tube running around the side of the boat). The sponson is in sections, so if one section is punctured, the others stay inflated. The sponson is covered with a tough nylon coating called Hypalon.

Flashing light beacon

Radar reflector

Starboard navigation light

Reflector support stanchion

Outboard motor

Outboard motor cover

Propeller

Outboard motor mounting bracket

VHF aerial

Inflatable righting airbag

Roll bar

General purpose rope

Lifeline

Inflatable sponson

Waterproof fuel tank

Helmsman

The helmsman sits in front of the other two crew members. By operating the steering wheel with the left hand and the motor controls with the right, the helmsman can immediately adjust the speed or direction of the lifeboat to suit the conditions at sea.

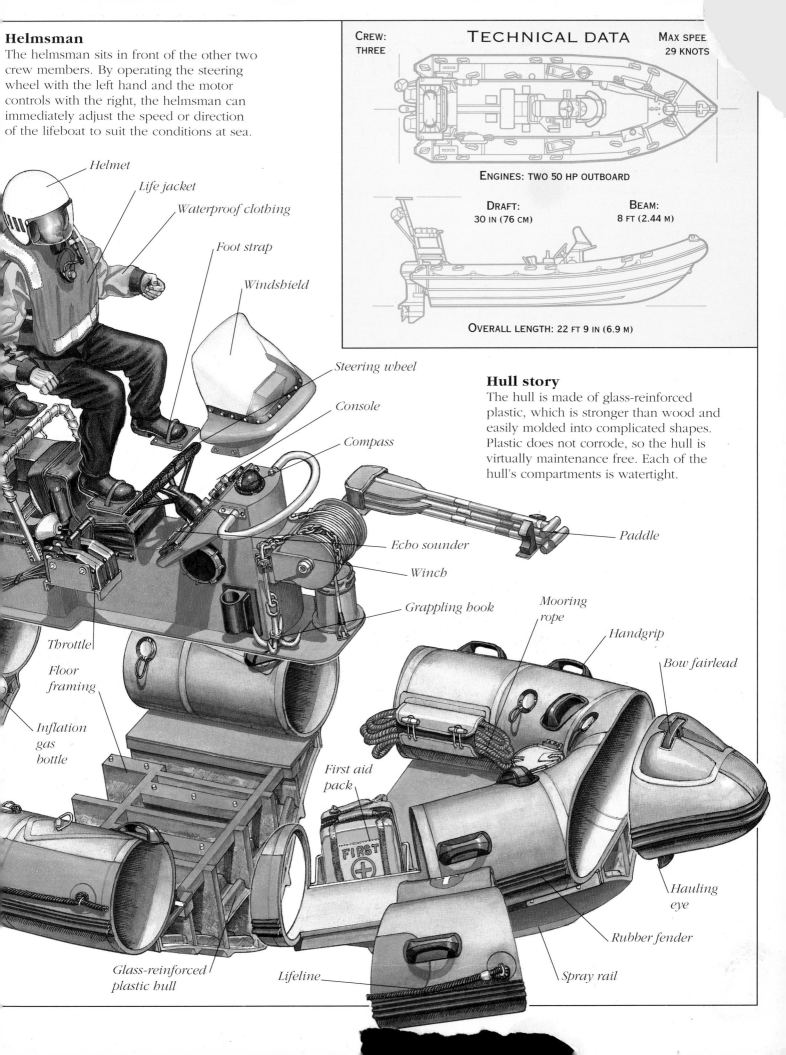

Helmet

Life jacket

Waterproof clothing

Foot strap

Windshield

Steering wheel

Console

Compass

Echo sounder

Winch

Grappling hook

Throttle

Floor framing

Inflation gas bottle

Paddle

Mooring rope

Handgrip

Bow fairlead

First aid pack

Hauling eye

Rubber fender

Spray rail

Glass-reinforced plastic hull

Lifeline

TECHNICAL DATA

CREW: THREE

MAX SPEE 29 KNOTS

ENGINES: TWO 50 HP OUTBOARD

DRAFT: 30 IN (76 CM)

BEAM: 8 FT (2.44 M)

OVERALL LENGTH: 22 FT 9 IN (6.9 M)

Hull story

The hull is made of glass-reinforced plastic, which is stronger than wood and easily molded into complicated shapes. Plastic does not corrode, so the hull is virtually maintenance free. Each of the hull's compartments is watertight.

SEA KING

Anticollision light

Blade pitch change mechanism

Rotor blade balancing weight

Radome (radar scanner cover)

THE DISTINCTIVE HIGH-visibility coloring of an air-sea rescue helicopter is just about the best sight in the world when you're shivering on the deck of a sinking ship, waiting to be rescued. Once winched to the safety of the helicopter, the injured are given emergency first aid and rushed at speeds of up to 155 mph (250 km/h) back to an air-sea rescue base. Originally developed as an anti-submarine weapon, this air-sea rescue helicopter, named the Sea King, is equipped with two Rolls-Royce Gnome turbine engines so that if one engine fails, the Sea King can still return to base using the other.

5-blade tail rotor (stops helicopter from spinning around)

Tail rotor driveshaft

Radar scanner

UHF aerial

Nonretractable tail wheel

Winch

Winch floodlight

Winch operator

Winched to safety
When it reaches the target, the Sea King is maneuvered to exactly the right position before the winch operator lowers the winchman on the end of a steel cable. The winch operator controls the winch from a panel alongside the door. The winchman picks up the person being rescued and together they are winched back up into the helicopter.

Swiveling seat mounting

Fuel tank

Sliding main door

Retractable starboard main landing gear

Bilge pump access covers

Steel winch cable

Stretcher

Stretcher
The Neil Robertson stretcher, named after its inventor, has cloth strips attached to it that are stiffened with splints. This arrangement immobilizes casualties until they are safe in a hospital.

Emergency flotation bag

Winchman

Starboard navigation light

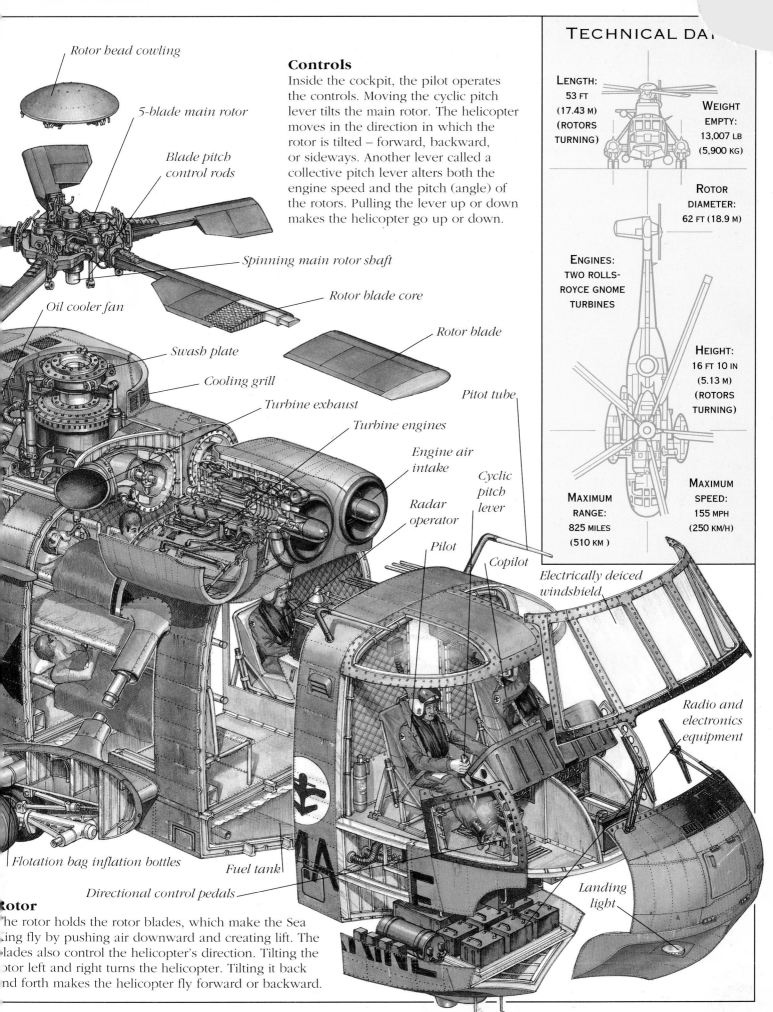

Rotor head cowling

5-blade main rotor

Blade pitch
control rods

Spinning main rotor shaft

Rotor blade core

Oil cooler fan

Swash plate

Rotor blade

Cooling grill

Turbine exhaust

Turbine engines

Pitot tube

Engine air
intake

Cyclic
pitch
lever

Radar
operator

Pilot

Copilot

Electrically deiced
windshield

Radio and
electronics
equipment

Flotation bag inflation bottles

Fuel tank

Directional control pedals

Landing
light

Controls

Inside the cockpit, the pilot operates the controls. Moving the cyclic pitch lever tilts the main rotor. The helicopter moves in the direction in which the rotor is tilted – forward, backward, or sideways. Another lever called a collective pitch lever alters both the engine speed and the pitch (angle) of the rotors. Pulling the lever up or down makes the helicopter go up or down.

Rotor

The rotor holds the rotor blades, which make the Sea King fly by pushing air downward and creating lift. The blades also control the helicopter's direction. Tilting the rotor left and right turns the helicopter. Tilting it back and forth makes the helicopter fly forward or backward.

LENGTH:
53 FT
(17.43 M)
(ROTORS
TURNING)

WEIGHT
EMPTY:
13,007 LB
(5,900 KG)

ROTOR
DIAMETER:
62 FT (18.9 M)

ENGINES:
TWO ROLLS-
ROYCE GNOME
TURBINES

HEIGHT:
16 FT 10 IN
(5.13 M)
(ROTORS
TURNING)

MAXIMUM
RANGE:
825 MILES
(510 KM)

MAXIMUM
SPEED:
155 MPH
(250 KM/H)

RANGE ROVER

SIX O' CLOCK ON A WINTER EVENING with freezing rain – the time and weather conditions that can easily lead to a major accident on a highway. As soon as a 911 call comes over the radio, police units are on the way to the scene driving all-weather vehicles. The Range Rover shown here is a workhorse for many police officers on patrol around the world. With its four-wheel drive and powerful engine, it can get around in all weather and help remove vehicles from the busy, dangerous lanes of a highway to the safety of the shoulder.

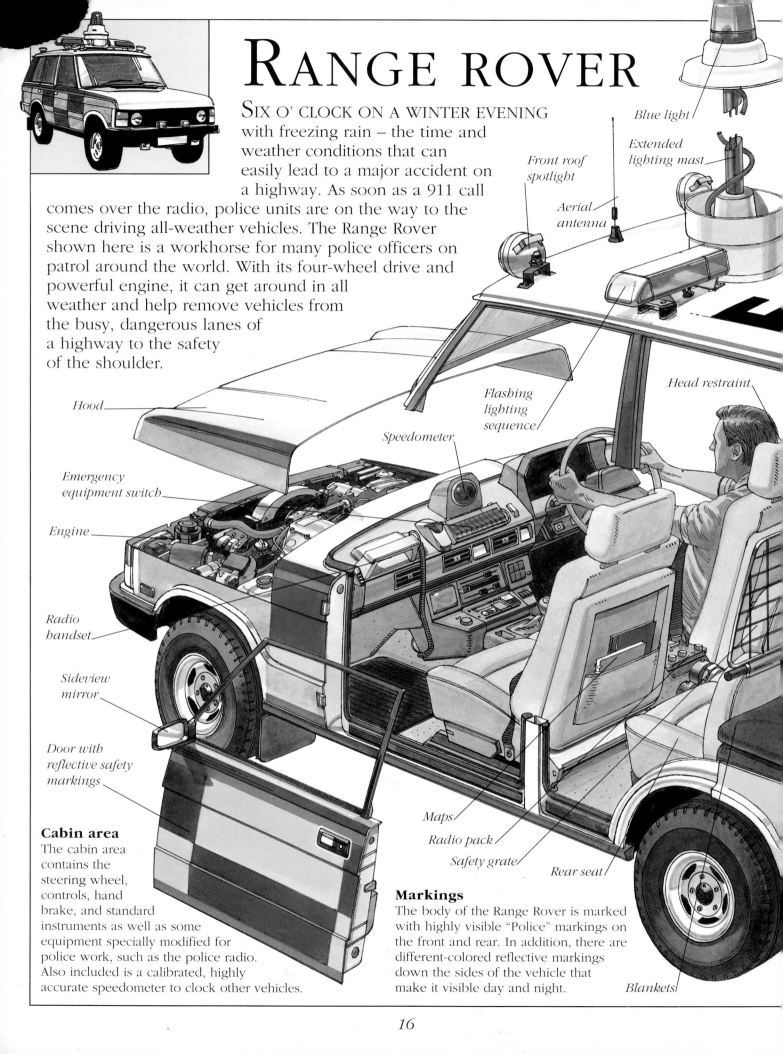

Blue light

Extended lighting mast

Front roof spotlight

Aerial antenna

Flashing lighting sequence

Speedometer

Head restraint

Hood

Emergency equipment switch

Engine

Radio handset

Sideview mirror

Door with reflective safety markings

Maps

Radio pack

Safety grate

Rear seat

Blankets

Cabin area
The cabin area contains the steering wheel, controls, hand brake, and standard instruments as well as some equipment specially modified for police work, such as the police radio. Also included is a calibrated, highly accurate speedometer to clock other vehicles.

Markings
The body of the Range Rover is marked with highly visible "Police" markings on the front and rear. In addition, there are different-colored reflective markings down the sides of the vehicle that make it visible day and night.

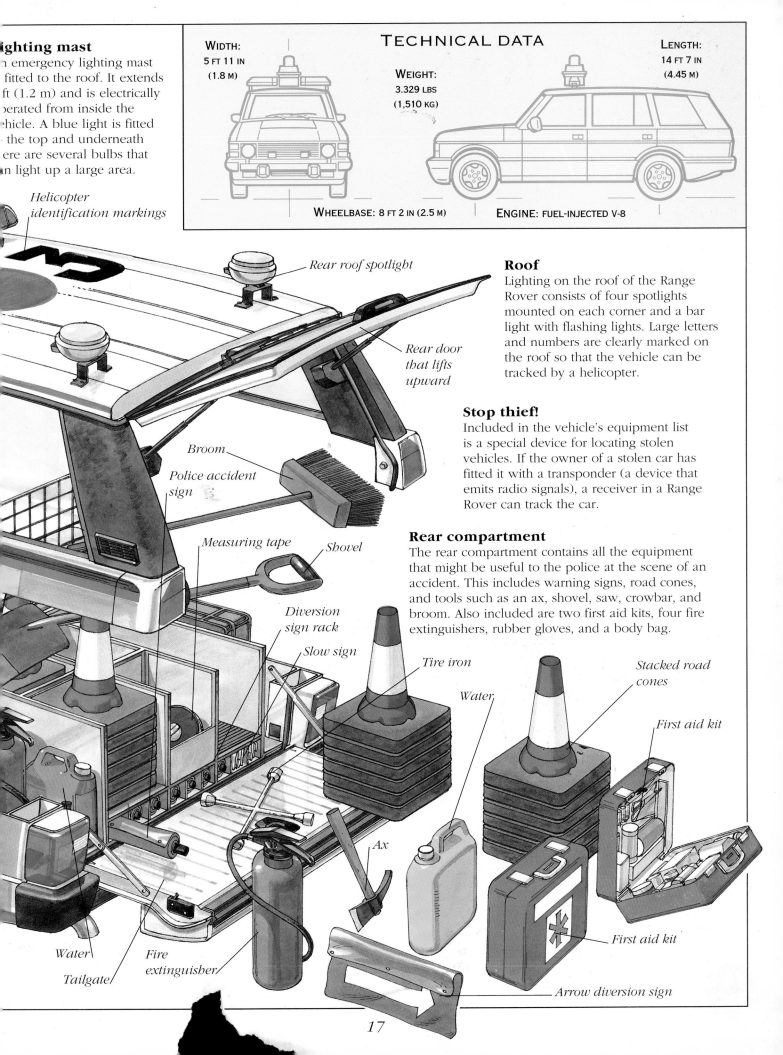

ighting mast

emergency lighting mast
fitted to the roof. It extends
ft (1.2 m) and is electrically
perated from inside the
hicle. A blue light is fitted
the top and underneath
ere are several bulbs that
light up a large area.

*Helicopter
identification markings*

TECHNICAL DATA

WIDTH:
5 FT 11 IN
(1.8 M)

WEIGHT:
3.329 LBS
(1,510 KG)

LENGTH:
14 FT 7 IN
(4.45 M)

WHEELBASE: 8 FT 2 IN (2.5 M)

ENGINE: FUEL-INJECTED V-8

Rear roof spotlight

*Rear door
that lifts
upward*

Broom

*Police accident
sign*

Measuring tape

Shovel

*Diversion
sign rack*

Slow sign

Tire iron

Water

*Stacked road
cones*

First aid kit

Ax

Water

Tailgate

*Fire
extinguisher*

First aid kit

Arrow diversion sign

Roof

Lighting on the roof of the Range
Rover consists of four spotlights
mounted on each corner and a bar
light with flashing lights. Large letters
and numbers are clearly marked on
the roof so that the vehicle can be
tracked by a helicopter.

Stop thief!

Included in the vehicle's equipment list
is a special device for locating stolen
vehicles. If the owner of a stolen car has
fitted it with a transponder (a device that
emits radio signals), a receiver in a Range
Rover can track the car.

Rear compartment

The rear compartment contains all the equipment
that might be useful to the police at the scene of an
accident. This includes warning signs, road cones,
and tools such as an ax, shovel, saw, crowbar, and
broom. Also included are two first aid kits, four fire
extinguishers, rubber gloves, and a body bag.

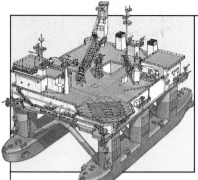

OILFIELD ESV

DAY IN AND DAY OUT ALL THROUGH the year, men and women are at work on offshore rigs drilling oil from beneath the seabed.

Usually things run smoothly, but sometimes disaster strikes. When it does, the crew of an Emergency Support Vessel swings into operation fighting fires, evacuating casualties, and diving deep underwater to plug blowouts. Helicopter pilots hover their craft above licking flames to winch workers to safety and fly them either to the ESV, where fully trained medical staff wait to treat the injured, or to shore. And all the time, the ESV must hold a steady position in often mountainous seas and howling winds.

The bridge

The captain of an ESV runs the vessel from the bridge, situated on the upper deck. All the ship's major functions are controlled from here, so it must have good all-around visibility to allow the crew to see what is happening all the time. The windows are specially designed to withstand heat and blasts.

Staying still

Onboard computers automatically adjust devices called thrusters that can move the ship very quickly to port, starboard, fore, or aft, and keep the vessel in the same position without having to drop anchor.

The rays above

Sailors use radar to locate the position of vessels at sea. The radar aerial sends out invisible rays. When these rays hit an object, they bounce off it back to a radar scanner on board the ship. The scanner relays the information to a screen in the navigator's station. The screen shows the distance the object is from the boat.

Aerial cluster

Fast rescue craft launch /recovery crane

Semirigid fast rescue craft

Radar scanner

Radar unit

Reinforced, heat-resistant windows

Bridge

Sikorsky S61N Puma helicopter or equivalent

Accommodations

Helicopter hangar

Lifeboat boom

Anchor

Mooring bitt

Thruster engine

Lifeboat

Thruster port

Lateral thrusters

Engine room

Anchor winch

Anchor chain

Anchor

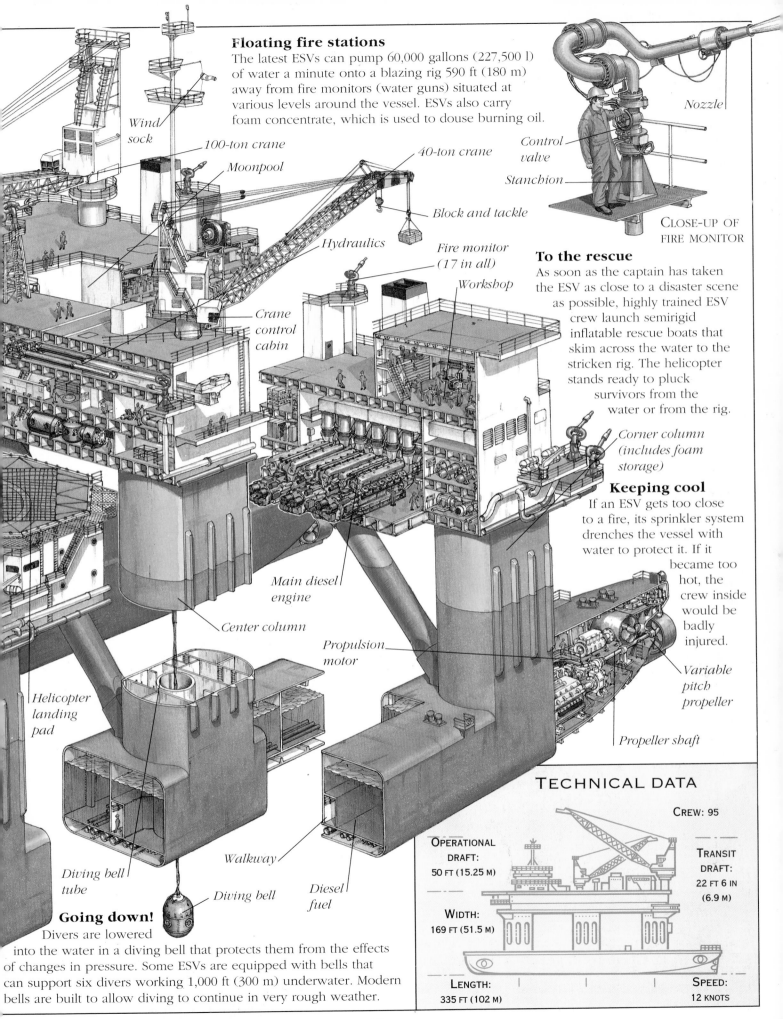

Floating fire stations

The latest ESVs can pump 60,000 gallons (227,500 l) of water a minute onto a blazing rig 590 ft (180 m) away from fire monitors (water guns) situated at various levels around the vessel. ESVs also carry foam concentrate, which is used to douse burning oil.

Wind sock

100-ton crane

Moonpool

40-ton crane

Block and tackle

Hydraulics

Crane control cabin

Fire monitor (17 in all)

Workshop

Nozzle

Control valve

Stanchion

CLOSE-UP OF FIRE MONITOR

To the rescue

As soon as the captain has taken the ESV as close to a disaster scene as possible, highly trained ESV crew launch semirigid inflatable rescue boats that skim across the water to the stricken rig. The helicopter stands ready to pluck survivors from the water or from the rig.

Corner column (includes foam storage)

Keeping cool

If an ESV gets too close to a fire, its sprinkler system drenches the vessel with water to protect it. If it became too hot, the crew inside would be badly injured.

Main diesel engine

Center column

Propulsion motor

Variable pitch propeller

Propeller shaft

Helicopter landing pad

Diving bell tube

Walkway

Diving bell

Diesel fuel

Going down!

Divers are lowered into the water in a diving bell that protects them from the effects of changes in pressure. Some ESVs are equipped with bells that can support six divers working 1,000 ft (300 m) underwater. Modern bells are built to allow diving to continue in very rough weather.

TECHNICAL DATA

CREW: 95

OPERATIONAL DRAFT: 50 FT (15.25 M)

TRANSIT DRAFT: 22 FT 6 IN (6.9 M)

WIDTH: 169 FT (51.5 M)

LENGTH: 335 FT (102 M)

SPEED: 12 KNOTS

LIFEBOAT

EARLY LIFEBOATS WERE OPEN to the wind and rain. The crew lashed themselves to their seats and rowed, in constant danger of capsizing, through towering waves and gale-force winds to rescue stricken sailors. Today's lifeboats, like this Trent class, are specially designed to skim to the rescue across the water and safely home again as quickly as possible. If they capsize, they right themselves immediately. Most coastal nations have special organizations to coordinate sea rescues. One of the oldest is Britain's Royal National Lifeboat Institution (RNLI), founded in 1824.

What's in a number?
You can tell something about a lifeboat by looking at the numbers painted on its side. The first set shows the boat's length in meters or feet, depending on where it was built. The second set shows whether it was the first, second, or even fifty-third of its class to be built.

Ring for safety
Life buoys will keep people who fall overboard afloat until they can be rescued, but they must be hauled to safety as soon as possible. If someone is in cold water for too long, their body temperature quickly drops to a point where death becomes likely.

Sea horsepower
The engine room is the heart of any lifeboat. Trent class lifeboats are powered by two diesel engines, each more powerful than 800 horses. The fuel tanks hold 1,083 gallons (4,100 l), which allows the boat to plow through the seas for more than 286 miles (460 km) before it has to be back in harbor.

Whip aerial antenna

Radar scanner

Direction finder

Coxswain

Emergency inflatable boat storage

Handrail

Life buoy

Steering gear access hatch

Towing fairlead

Portable fire pump

Engine exhaust pipe

Rudder

Propeller

Fiber-reinforced composite hull

Engine room

Engine

Pressure gauge

Fast floaters
Newer and newer lifeboats are increasingly easy to maintain and have maximum speeds of up to 25 knots.

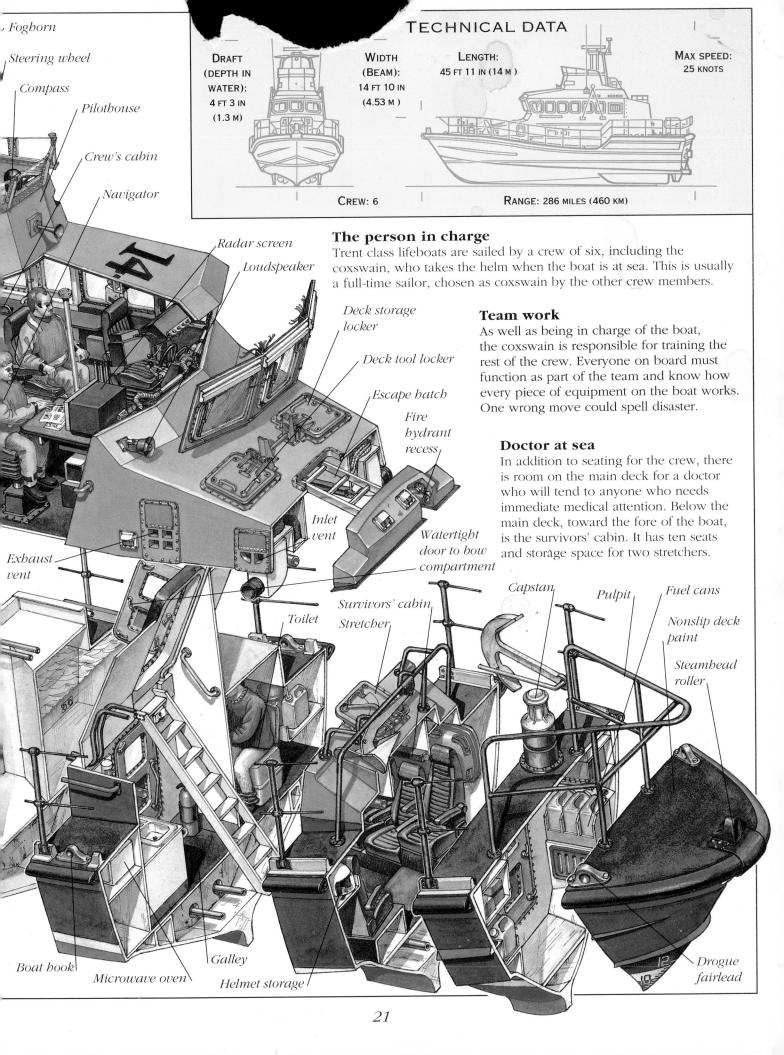

Foghorn

Steering wheel

Compass

Pilothouse

Crew's cabin

Navigator

Radar screen

Loudspeaker

Deck storage locker

Deck tool locker

Escape hatch

Fire hydrant recess

Inlet vent

Exhaust vent

Watertight door to bow compartment

Boat hook

Microwave oven

Galley

Toilet

Helmet storage

Survivors' cabin

Stretcher

Capstan

Pulpit

Fuel cans

Nonslip deck paint

Steamhead roller

Drogue fairlead

The person in charge

Trent class lifeboats are sailed by a crew of six, including the coxswain, who takes the helm when the boat is at sea. This is usually a full-time sailor, chosen as coxswain by the other crew members.

Team work

As well as being in charge of the boat, the coxswain is responsible for training the rest of the crew. Everyone on board must function as part of the team and know how every piece of equipment on the boat works. One wrong move could spell disaster.

Doctor at sea

In addition to seating for the crew, there is room on the main deck for a doctor who will tend to anyone who needs immediate medical attention. Below the main deck, toward the fore of the boat, is the survivors' cabin. It has ten seats and storage space for two stretchers.

AMBULANCE

FOR AN ACCIDENT OR HEART ATTACK VICTIM, a few minutes without medical aid can mean the difference between life and death. That's why modern ambulances are like mini-hospitals on wheels. The ambulance shown here is packed with lifesaving equipment. Rushing to the scene of an emergency at high speed, it carries a crew trained in the latest lifesaving techniques. After the victims have been stabilized, the ambulance rushes them to the nearest hospital.

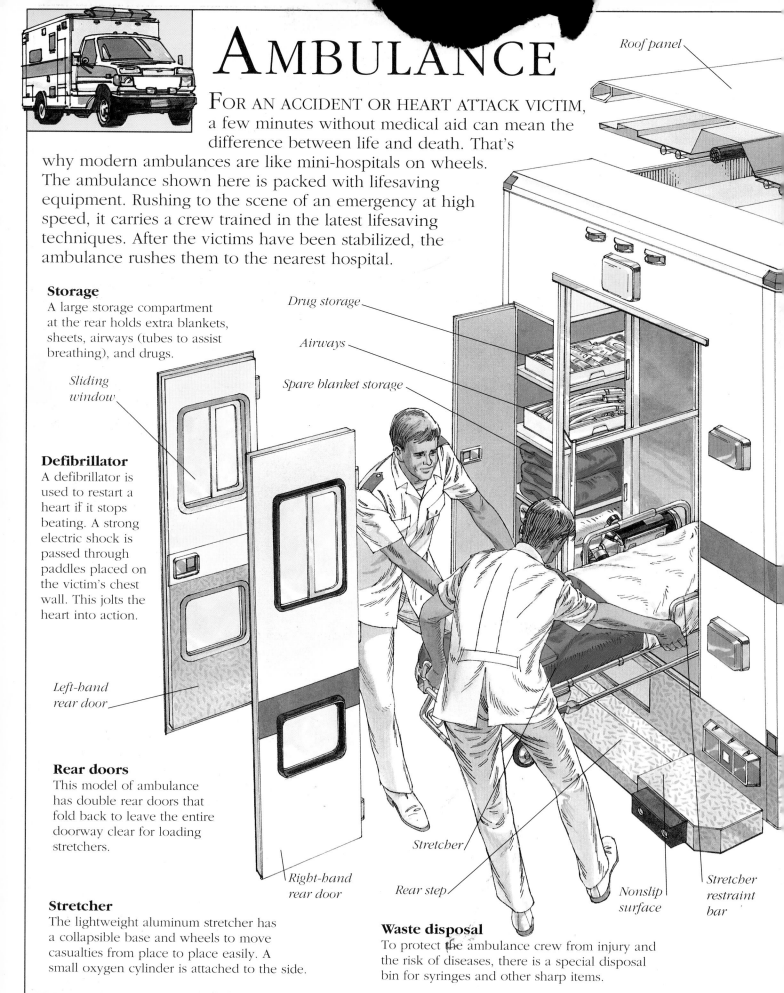

Roof panel

Storage
A large storage compartment at the rear holds extra blankets, sheets, airways (tubes to assist breathing), and drugs.

Drug storage

Airways

Spare blanket storage

Sliding window

Defibrillator
A defibrillator is used to restart a heart if it stops beating. A strong electric shock is passed through paddles placed on the victim's chest wall. This jolts the heart into action.

Left-hand rear door

Rear doors
This model of ambulance has double rear doors that fold back to leave the entire doorway clear for loading stretchers.

Right-hand rear door

Stretcher

Rear step

Nonslip surface

Stretcher restraint bar

Stretcher
The lightweight aluminum stretcher has a collapsible base and wheels to move casualties from place to place easily. A small oxygen cylinder is attached to the side.

Waste disposal
To protect the ambulance crew from injury and the risk of diseases, there is a special disposal bin for syringes and other sharp items.

22

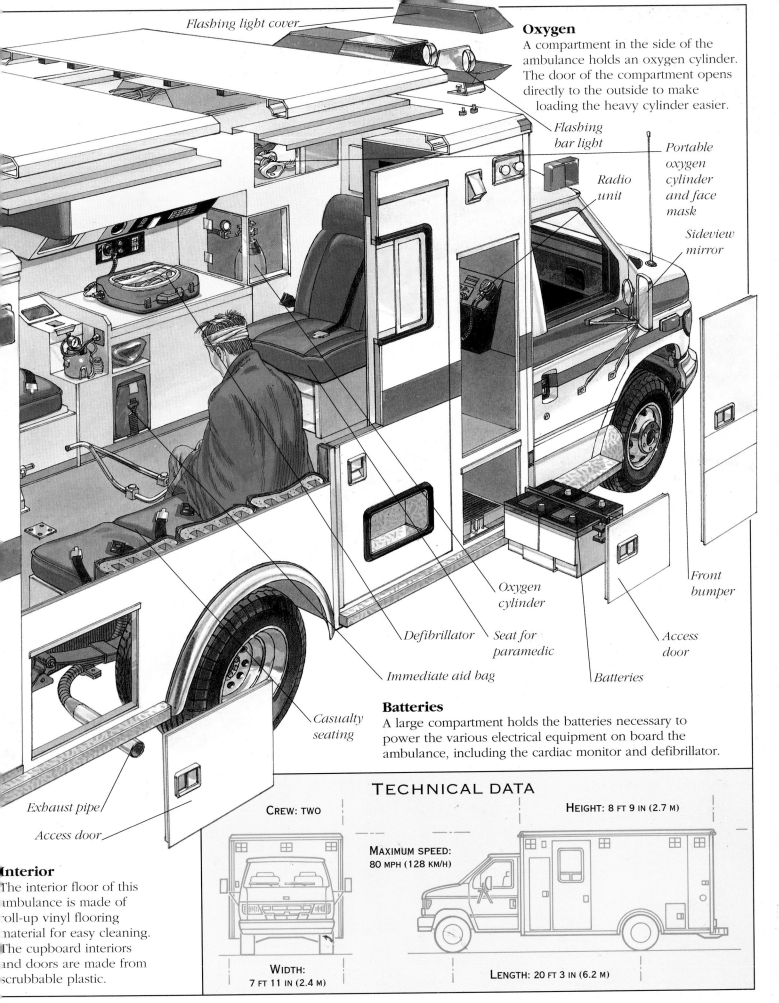

Flashing light cover

Oxygen
A compartment in the side of the ambulance holds an oxygen cylinder. The door of the compartment opens directly to the outside to make loading the heavy cylinder easier.

Flashing bar light

Radio unit

Portable oxygen cylinder and face mask

Sideview mirror

Oxygen cylinder

Defibrillator

Seat for paramedic

Access door

Front bumper

Immediate aid bag

Batteries

Casualty seating

Batteries
A large compartment holds the batteries necessary to power the various electrical equipment on board the ambulance, including the cardiac monitor and defibrillator.

Exhaust pipe

Access door

Interior
The interior floor of this ambulance is made of roll-up vinyl flooring material for easy cleaning. The cupboard interiors and doors are made from scrubbable plastic.

TECHNICAL DATA

CREW: TWO

HEIGHT: 8 FT 9 IN (2.7 M)

MAXIMUM SPEED: 80 MPH (128 KM/H)

WIDTH: 7 FT 11 IN (2.4 M)

LENGTH: 20 FT 3 IN (6.2 M)

PARAMEDIC BIKE

IN SOME COUNTRIES, you might see a paramedic motorcycle weaving in and out of the traffic in congested city streets. With its blue lights flashing and its siren wailing, a paramedic motorcycle can get to the scene of an accident in those vital few minutes before an ambulance struggles through a traffic jam or crowd of people. Equipped with a full medical kit, paramedic motorcyclists can treat almost any kind of injury.

First ones

The first paramedic bikes to be seen on British roads were brought into use by the West Midlands Ambulance Service in April 1990.

Keeping in touch

The rider keeps in radio contact with the ambulance via a headset situated in the rider's helmet. There is also a handheld portable radio that makes it possible to stay in touch even when the paramedic is away from the bike. As well as keeping the ambulance workers informed of the current situation, the paramedic can cancel the ambulance trip if the emergency call is a hoax.

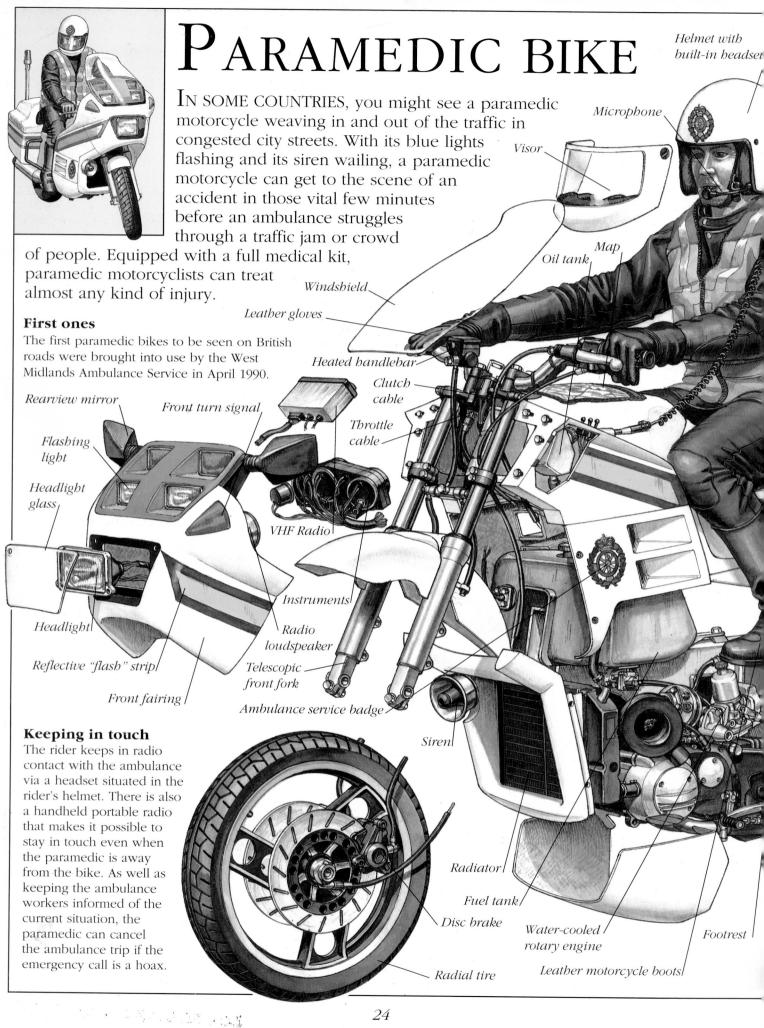

Helmet with built-in headset

Microphone

Visor

Map

Oil tank

Windshield

Leather gloves

Heated handlebar

Clutch cable

Throttle cable

Rearview mirror

Front turn signal

Flashing light

Headlight glass

VHF Radio

Instruments

Radio loudspeaker

Headlight

Telescopic front fork

Reflective "flash" strip

Ambulance service badge

Front fairing

Siren

Radiator

Fuel tank

Disc brake

Water-cooled rotary engine

Footrest

Radial tire

Leather motorcycle boots

Anti freeze

The motorcycle used by paramedics is the Norton Commander, adapted for paramedical use. One important modification is the heated handlebars. This is not to pamper the riders, but rather to ensure that their hands are not too cold to give first aid when they reach the scene.

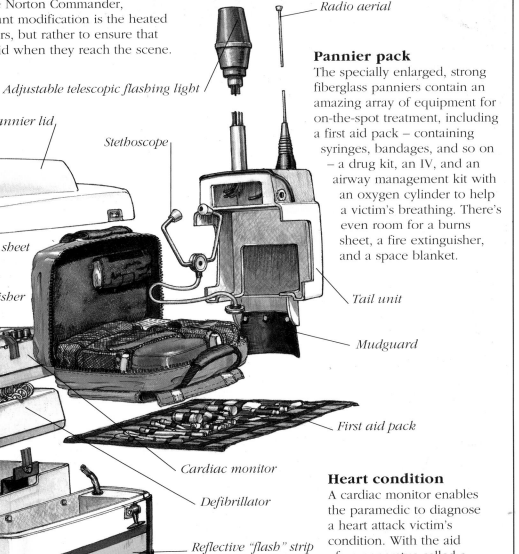

Leather jacket

High-visibility waterproof jacket

Space blanket

Saddle

Leather pants

Radio aerial

Adjustable telescopic flashing light

Pannier lid

Stethoscope

Pannier pack

The specially enlarged, strong fiberglass panniers contain an amazing array of equipment for on-the-spot treatment, including a first aid pack – containing syringes, bandages, and so on – a drug kit, an IV, and an airway management kit with an oxygen cylinder to help a victim's breathing. There's even room for a burns sheet, a fire extinguisher, and a space blanket.

Burns sheet

Fire extinguisher

Tail unit

Mudguard

First aid pack

Cardiac monitor

Defibrillator

Heart condition

A cardiac monitor enables the paramedic to diagnose a heart attack victim's condition. With the aid of an apparatus called a defibrillator – which sends an electric current to the chest wall – the paramedic can get the heart beating regularly again.

Reflective "flash" strip

Detachable metal pannier

Heat shield on inside

Adjustable rear suspension

Exhaust pipe end

Exhaust

Qualifications

The paramedics are super-skilled ambulance workers. They have advanced first aid skills, special motorcycle training, and maintain a top level of fitness.

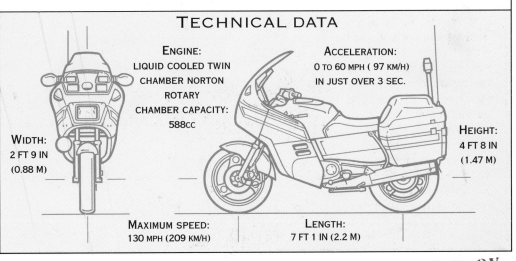

TECHNICAL DATA

ENGINE:
LIQUID COOLED TWIN CHAMBER NORTON ROTARY
CHAMBER CAPACITY: 588CC

ACCELERATION:
0 TO 60 MPH (97 KM/H)
IN JUST OVER 3 SEC.

WIDTH:
2 FT 9 IN
(0.88 M)

HEIGHT:
4 FT 8 IN
(1.47 M)

MAXIMUM SPEED:
130 MPH (209 KM/H)

LENGTH:
7 FT 1 IN (2.2 M)

WATER BOMBER

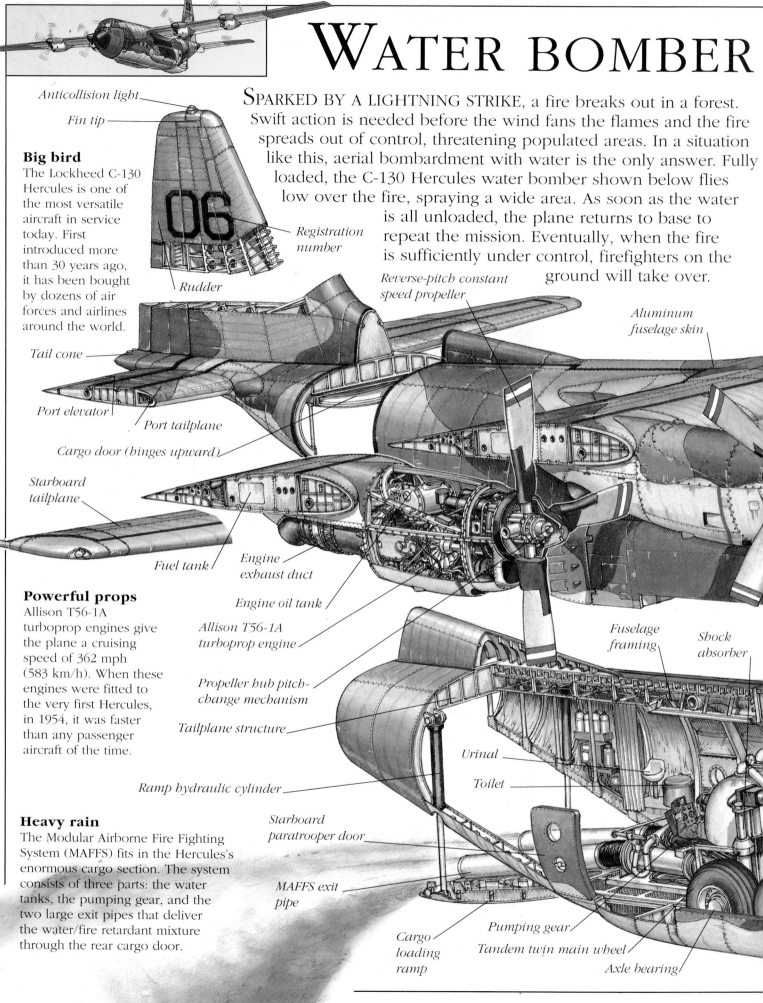

Fin tip

Big bird
The Lockheed C-130 Hercules is one of the most versatile aircraft in service today. First introduced more than 30 years ago, it has been bought by dozens of air forces and airlines around the world.

SPARKED BY A LIGHTNING STRIKE, a fire breaks out in a forest. Swift action is needed before the wind fans the flames and the fire spreads out of control, threatening populated areas. In a situation like this, aerial bombardment with water is the only answer. Fully loaded, the C-130 Hercules water bomber shown below flies low over the fire, spraying a wide area. As soon as the water is all unloaded, the plane returns to base to repeat the mission. Eventually, when the fire is sufficiently under control, firefighters on the ground will take over.

Registration number

Rudder

Reverse-pitch constant speed propeller

Aluminum fuselage skin

Tail cone

Port elevator

Port tailplane

Cargo door (hinges upward)

Starboard tailplane

Fuel tank

Engine exhaust duct

Engine oil tank

Powerful props
Allison T56-1A turboprop engines give the plane a cruising speed of 362 mph (583 km/h). When these engines were fitted to the very first Hercules, in 1954, it was faster than any passenger aircraft of the time.

Allison T56-1A turboprop engine

Propeller hub pitch-change mechanism

Tailplane structure

Fuselage framing

Shock absorber

Urinal

Toilet

Ramp hydraulic cylinder

Heavy rain
The Modular Airborne Fire Fighting System (MAFFS) fits in the Hercules's enormous cargo section. The system consists of three parts: the water tanks, the pumping gear, and the two large exit pipes that deliver the water/fire retardant mixture through the rear cargo door.

Starboard paratrooper door

MAFFS exit pipe

Cargo loading ramp

Pumping gear

Tandem twin main wheel

Axle bearing

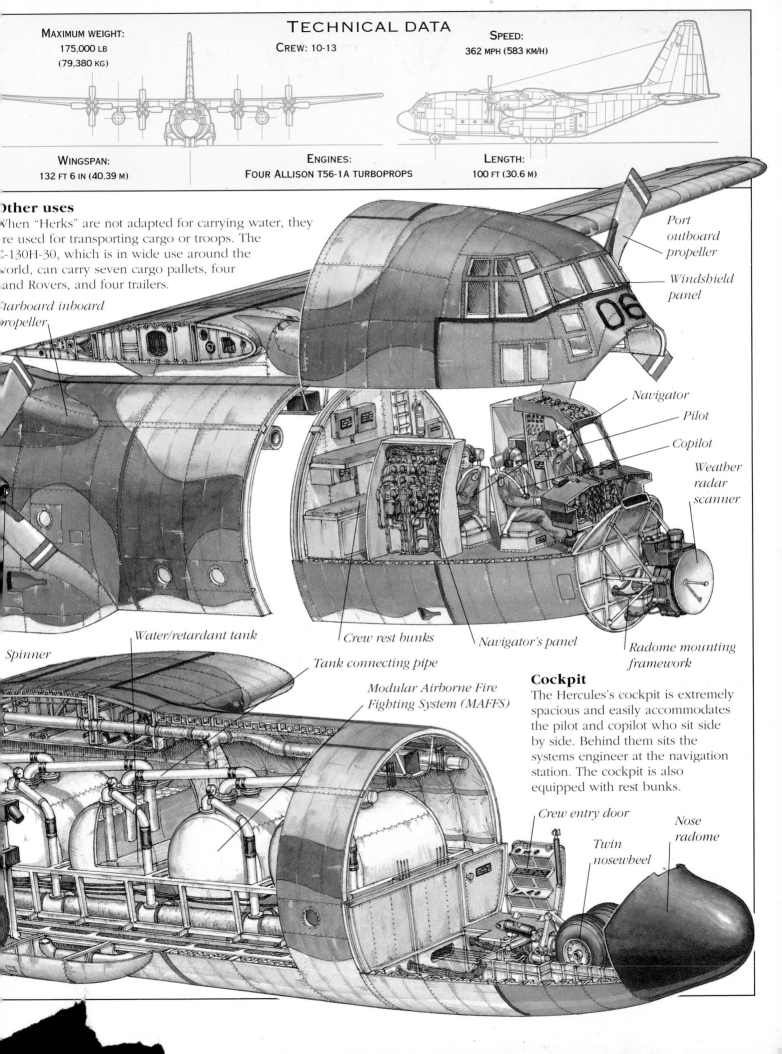

TECHNICAL DATA

MAXIMUM WEIGHT:
175,000 LB
(79,380 KG)

CREW: 10-13

SPEED:
362 MPH (583 KM/H)

WINGSPAN:
132 FT 6 IN (40.39 M)

ENGINES:
FOUR ALLISON T56-1A TURBOPROPS

LENGTH:
100 FT (30.6 M)

Other uses

When "Herks" are not adapted for carrying water, they are used for transporting cargo or troops. The C-130H-30, which is in wide use around the world, can carry seven cargo pallets, four Land Rovers, and four trailers.

Starboard inboard propeller

Port outboard propeller

Windshield panel

06

Navigator

Pilot

Copilot

Weather radar scanner

Crew rest bunks

Navigator's panel

Radome mounting framework

Spinner

Water/retardant tank

Tank connecting pipe

Modular Airborne Fire Fighting System (MAFFS)

Cockpit

The Hercules's cockpit is extremely spacious and easily accommodates the pilot and copilot who sit side by side. Behind them sits the systems engineer at the navigation station. The cockpit is also equipped with rest bunks.

Crew entry door

Twin nosewheel

Nose radome

HISTORICAL RESCUE

WHAT DO YOU DO IN AN EMERGENCY? Dial 911 and ask for the emergency service you need – and you expect a rapid response with appropriate aid. We take these things for granted, but in the days before telephone and radio, raising the alarm took time. In the event of a fire, a child was sent running to the fire station. Lifeboat crews were alerted by a gunshot. In those days, fire engines, ambulances, and police wagons were all horse-drawn – so it could take a very long time for rescuers to reach the scene. Add to that the fact that the crews were often poorly trained and equipped, and it makes you realize how lucky we are to have modern emergency services.

Funnel

Steam chest

Shand Mason fire engine
The steam fire engine was invented in 1829. A common sight in late Victorian cities, this example was built by the firm of Shand Mason. It took almost 10 minutes to build up enough steam to force a jet of water up to 90 ft (27.4 m) onto a fire.

Boiler

Water jet

Pumping handle

Air pressure vessel

Flywheel

Cylinder rods

Hand pumped early engine
This hand pumped fire engine was made around 1800. With a handle at either end, it needed two people to operate it. One advantage was its compact size – it was small enough to pull inside a house to fight a fire, if required.

Water intake from river or pond

Stoking platform

Fire hose

Boiler auxiliary water tank

Water pump

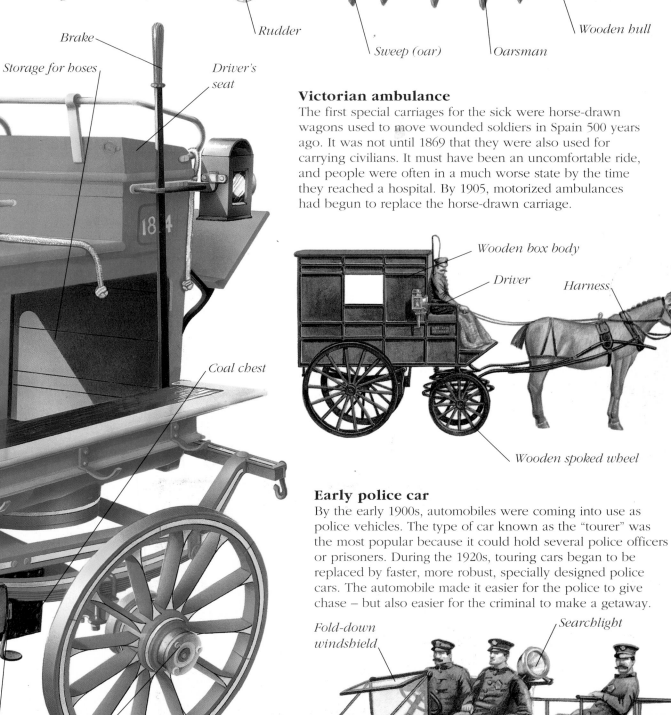

Early lifeboat

Until the 1780s ordinary fishing boats were
towed out in all seas to rescue shipwrecked
sailors. Then, in 1790, the first vessel specially
designed for lifesaving was built. These early
lifeboats were powered by oars and fitted
with sails for use in rougher conditions.

Helmsman (steers the boat)

Rudder

Sweep (oar)

Oarsman

Wooden hull

Brake

Storage for hoses

Driver's seat

Coal chest

Brake

Wheel hub

Wheel rim

Steel tire

Victorian ambulance

The first special carriages for the sick were horse-drawn
wagons used to move wounded soldiers in Spain 500 years
ago. It was not until 1869 that they were also used for
carrying civilians. It must have been an uncomfortable ride,
and people were often in a much worse state by the time
they reached a hospital. By 1905, motorized ambulances
had begun to replace the horse-drawn carriage.

Wooden box body

Driver

Harness

Wooden spoked wheel

Early police car

By the early 1900s, automobiles were coming into use as
police vehicles. The type of car known as the "tourer" was
the most popular because it could hold several police officers
or prisoners. During the 1920s, touring cars began to be
replaced by faster, more robust, specially designed police
cars. The automobile made it easier for the police to give
chase – but also easier for the criminal to make a getaway.

Fold-down windshield

Searchlight

Body based on touring car

Rear seats hold up to 6 officers

GLOSSARY

Aft
Toward the rear of a ship or aircraft.

Air-sea rescue
Rescuing victims at sea by helicopter.

AIR-SEA RESCUE

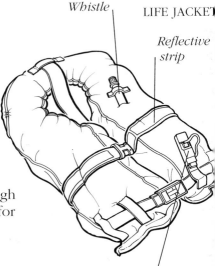

Winch operator

Sea King helicopter

Steel winch cable

Winchman with survivor

Airway
A tube that is inserted into someone's throat and down the windpipe to help them breathe.

Anchor
A heavy weight on the end of a rope or chain. It is thrown over the side of a ship and sticks in the seabed to stop the ship from moving.

Bar light
The emergency flashing light sequence on the roof of a rescue vehicle.

Bow
The front of a ship.

Bridge
An enclosed platform where the captain and helmsman stand on a ship. The ship is navigated and orders are given from here.

Bulkhead
A solid partition that separates one part of an aircraft or ship from another.

Cabin
Living quarters for someone on board a ship.

Capsize
When a boat turns upside down in the water.

Cardiac monitor
A machine that registers a patient's heartbeat on a screen. Pads called electrodes are attached to the patient to pick up the heartbeat.

CARDIAC MONITOR

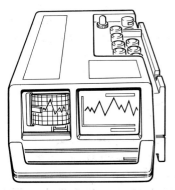

Compass
A device for finding the way. It consists of a magnetized needle that always points north.

Coxswain
The captain of a lifeboat.

Deck
A platform that stretches across and along a boat.

Defibrillator
A device that delivers an electric shock to a heart attack victim's chest wall to restart their heart when it has stopped.

Diving bell
A pressurized capsule that lowers divers down to the seabed. The divers use the bell as a temporary workstation on the seabed.

Emergency Support Vessel
A large, riglike vessel that can put out oil well fires and make repairs to drilling rigs.

Fuselage
The body of an airplane or helicopter.

Forward
Toward the front of a ship or aircraft.

Helicopter
An aircraft that uses spinning blades to create lift and fly through the air. It can be used for rescue work.

Helipad
A specially made landing place for a helicopter.

Helmsman
The crew member who steers a boat.

Hover
When a flying helicopter stays in one place, for example while rescuing a casualty.

Hull
The main body of a boat – the part that sits in the water.

K-9 division
A division of a police force that uses dogs to assist police officers in combating crime.

Keel
A strong rib that runs all the way along underneath a ship's hull. It is the backbone of the ship.

Life jacket
A lifesaving device that straps onto the body to keep people afloat in water. It is filled with air or material that floats, such as plastic foam.

Whistle

LIFE JACKET

Reflective strip

Seawater-activated battery light

Lifeboat
A small boat with powerful engines used to rescue people in trouble at sea. Most lifeboats are self-righting – if they capsize in bad weather, they immediately turn right side up again.

Monitor
A powerful water cannon used to put out fires.

Moonpool
A hole in the middle of the deck of a ship. It is used to lower heavy equipment to the seabed.

Pilot
The person who operates an aircraft.

Port
The left-hand side of a ship or aircraft.

Propeller
Blades mounted on a shaft that propel an aircraft or ship by pushing on air or water.

STRETCHERS

Lifting harness

Ambulance stretcher

Oxygen cylinder

Neil Robertson stretcher
A stretcher, named after its inventor, that has wooden splints to keep a casualty immobile until they reach a hospital.

Paramedic
An ambulance worker who has undertaken extra training in emergency lifesaving techniques. Paramedics stabilize casualties until they can be taken to a hospital.

1824, it is the oldest organization for saving lives at sea.

Rotor
The device on the top of a helicopter that holds the rotor blades and whirls them around, creating lift.

Basket stretcher

Radar
Radio Detection and Ranging: the navigation system that uses beams of directed radio waves to locate objects.

RNLI
The Royal National Lifeboat Institution of Great Britain. Founded in

Rotor blade
One of the long wing-shaped structures attached to the rotor of a helicopter.

Satellite navigation
A navigation system used by ships at sea that relies on satellites to determine exact positions.

Rudder
A metal structure at the rear of a ship or aircraft that is turned to make the craft go left or right.

Self-righting device
A system on lifeboats that uses shifting tanks of water or air bags to turn the boat right side up if it capsizes.

Stretcher
A flat, rectangular frame for moving a casualty from the scene of an accident to a hospital.

Wooden splints

Neil Robertson stretcher

Safety rail

Winchman
The crew member on board a helicopter who is lowered on a cable to rescue someone.

WINCHMAN

Safety helmet

Cable

Casualty

INDEX

Acknowledgments

Dorling Kindersley would like
to thank the following people
who helped in the preparation
of this book:

Additional artwork by Alan
Austin (pages 6-7, 16-17, 22-23)
Blue Chip (pages 10-11) and
David Gillingwater (pages 28-29)
Line artwork by Gary Biggin
and John See
Additional text by Moira
Butterfield and Michael
Johnstone
Lynn Bresler for the index

Also
Angloco Limited
BP Exploration UK Limited
Royal National Lifeboat
Institution
Sgt. Keith L. Worger, Surrey
Police Mobile Support Division.